VELOCIRAPTOR

LEIGH ROCKWOOD

PowerKiDS press™

New York

To Christopher and the one pound, twelve ounce baby Velociraptor he named, Botanicus. 11/8/10, a day we will never forget! - KL

Published in 2012 by The Rosen Publishing Group, Inc.
29 East 21st Street, New York, NY 10010

First Edition

Editor: Joanne Randolph
Book Design: Kate Laczynski

Photo Credits: Cover, title page by Brian Garvey; cover background (palm tree leaves) © www.iStockphoto.com/dra_schwartz; cover background (palm tree trunk) iStockphoto/Thinkstock; cover background (ginkgo leaves) Hemera/Thinkstock; cover background (fern leaves) Brand X Pictures/Thinkstock; cover background (moss texture) © www.iStockphoto.com/Robert Linton; pp. 4, 5, 6, 7, 8, 10, 11 (left), 12–13, 14, 16, 17, 18–19, 20–21, 22; p. 9 © www.iStockpoto.com/Viktor Glupov; p. 11 (right) © www.iStockphoto.com/Jim Jurica; p. 15 © www.iStockphoto.com/Jeff Chiasson.

Library of Congress Cataloging-in-Publication Data

Rockwood, Leigh.
  Velociraptor / by Leigh Rockwood. — 1st ed.
      p. cm. — (Dinosaurs ruled!)
  Includes index.
  ISBN 978-1-4488-4968-0 (library binding) — ISBN 978-1-4488-5086-0 (pbk.) — ISBN 978-1-4488-5087-7 (6-pack)
  1. Velociraptor—Juvenile literature. I. Title. II. Series.
  QE862.S3R5556 2012
  567.912—dc22

                            2010051378

Manufactured in the United States of America

CPSIA Compliance Information: Batch #WS11PK: For Further Information contact Rosen Publishing, New York, New York at 1-800-237-9932

CONTENTS

MEET THE VELOCIRAPTOR

The velociraptor was a small, quick, two-footed dinosaur. It had a sharp claw on each foot to help it kill its **prey**. This dinosaur's quickness helped earn it the name velociraptor, which means "speedy thief."

Paleontologists have learned these facts and more by studying velociraptor **fossils**. Even though

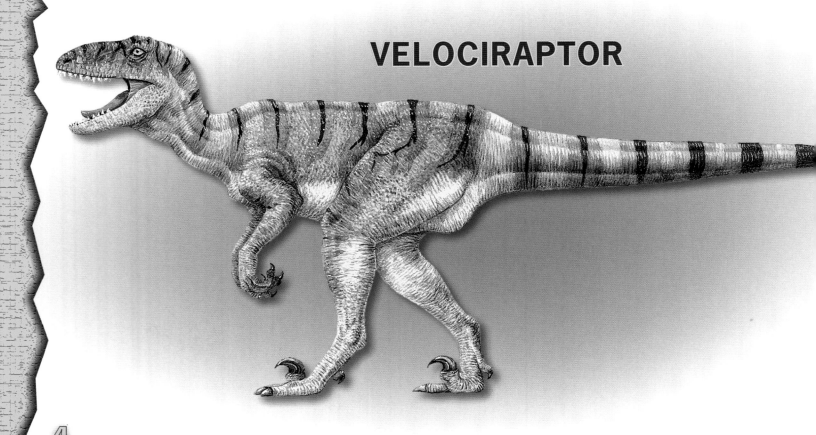

VELOCIRAPTOR

The velociraptor was a hunter. Here you can see its special toe, which it held up off the ground. It likely used the claw on this toe to hurt or kill its prey.

this dinosaur has been **extinct** for millions of years, its fossils give scientists clues about its life. These clues help scientists come up with theories, or ideas, about what the velociraptor ate, how it lived, and how it died.

THE LATE CRETACEOUS PERIOD

Dinosaurs lived for over 100 million years. This period is just a small part of the 4.5 billion years Earth has existed. Scientists use a system called geologic time to organize Earth's long history. The velociraptor lived during the Late Cretaceous period, which lasted from about 89 to 65 million years ago. The velociraptor preyed on plant-eating dinosaurs such as the protoceratops.

Velociraptors and their relatives hunted plant eaters such as the tenontosaurus. They sometimes hunted in packs.

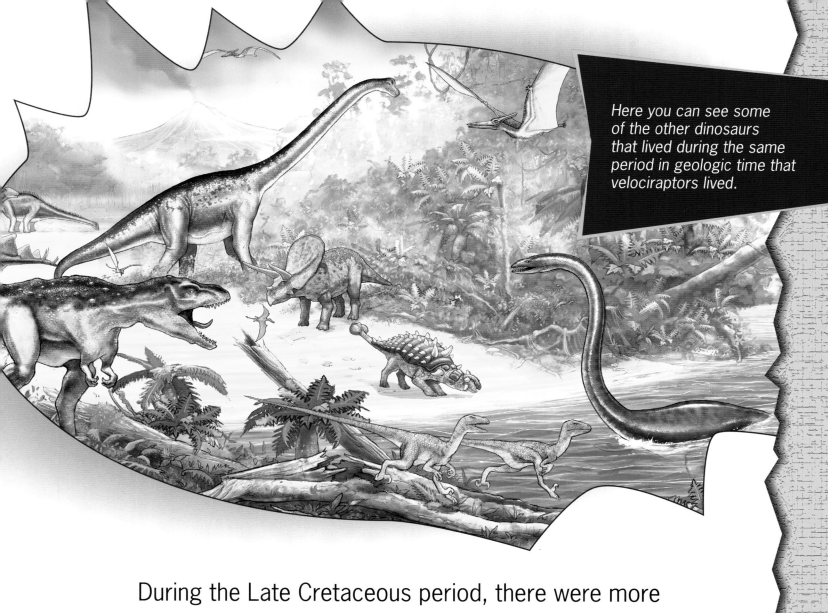

Here you can see some of the other dinosaurs that lived during the same period in geologic time that velociraptors lived.

During the Late Cretaceous period, there were more dinosaurs and more dinosaur **species** than at any other time. Dinosaurs died out in a mass extinction at the end of this period. Paleontologists think the mass extinction could have been due to volcanic activity, asteroids hitting Earth, or climate change.

WHERE DID THE VELOCIRAPTOR LIVE?

The velociraptor lived in parts of what is now China, Mongolia, and Russia. This land is rich in many species of dinosaur fossils. Paleontologists think millions of years ago huge rainstorms here caused sand dunes to collapse. The falling sand killed many dinosaurs and buried them before other animals could eat them.

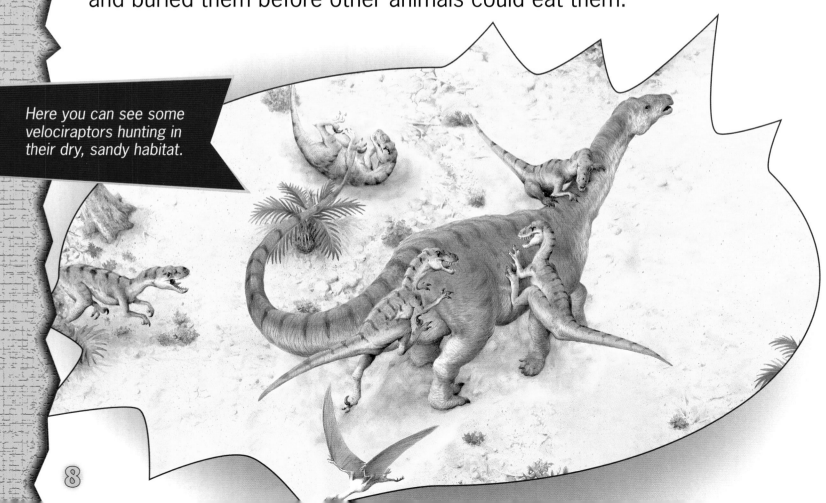

Here you can see some velociraptors hunting in their dry, sandy habitat.

Many dinosaur fossils, including those of velociraptors, have been found in the rocks of these canyons in the Gobi Desert.

Over time this sand pressed together and formed **sedimentary rocks**. The dinosaurs' bodies fossilized.

During the Late Cretaceous period, the lands where the velociraptor lived were hot and dry. Today some of these lands are part of the Gobi Desert, in Asia. This desert is dry but often much colder than other deserts around the world.

THE VELOCIRAPTOR'S BODY

The velociraptor was a small, fast **predator**. An adult's body was around 6 feet (2 m) long from head to tail, 3 feet (1 m) tall, and about 30 pounds (14 kg) in weight. This dinosaur ran on its back legs and likely could run about 40 miles per hour (60 km/h)!

The velociraptor ran with its tail held straight out behind it. It was fast, which helped it catch its food.

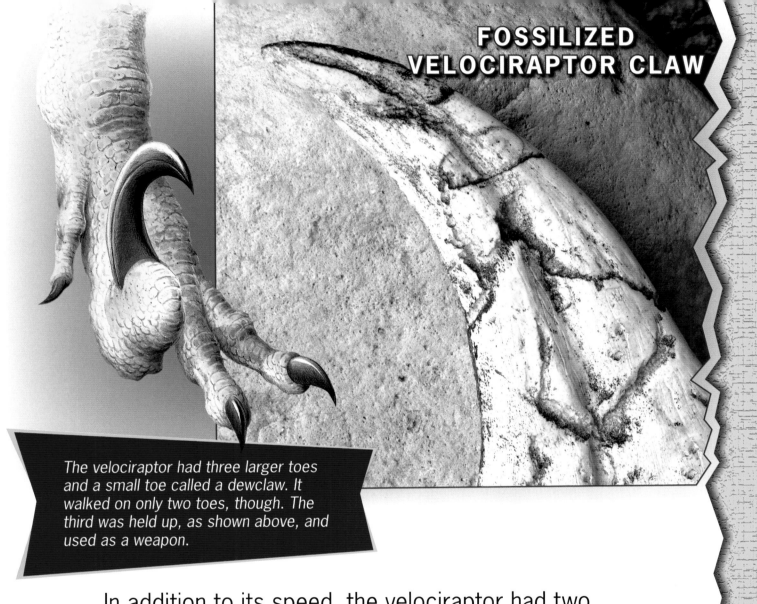

The velociraptor had three larger toes and a small toe called a dewclaw. It walked on only two toes, though. The third was held up, as shown above, and used as a weapon.

In addition to its speed, the velociraptor had two other weapons for hunting its prey. First, it had a 3.5-inch-(9 cm) long **retractable** claw on each foot. This claw may have been used to hurt its prey. The velociraptor also had a mouth full of about 80 sharp teeth, with which it could tear into its prey.

A FINE, FEATHERED DINOSAUR

Can you picture a dinosaur with feathers? Scientists now know that the velociraptor had feathers. Paleontologists know this from looking at the fossilized bones of its front limbs. There they could see quill knobs, which are the places where feathers were connected to the bone by **ligaments**. The fact that some dinosaurs had feathers shows us that dinosaurs are relatives of today's birds as well as lizards.

Even though it did not fly, the velociraptor's feathers could have served other purposes. Feathers may have helped the dinosaur control its body temperature. Bright feathers also could have helped males draw **mates** to them!

Velociraptors belonged to a group called dromaeosaurs, which were generally feathered, birdlike dinosaurs.

DINO BITE

The velociraptor had hollow bones. This is something that it had in common with today's birds.

13

A SHARP MIND

The velociraptor's head was about 7 inches (18 cm) long. This may not sound big, but it did have a large head compared to the size of its body. Scientists measure dinosaurs' intelligence by comparing the size of a dinosaur's skull against the size of its body. This means that the velociraptor is thought to be one of the smartest dinosaurs that ever lived.

Velociraptors and other dromaeosaurs had large skulls compared to their overall size.

The velociraptor had binocular vision. This means that both of its eyes faced forward and could focus on the same thing at once. Binocular vision lets animals see how far away things are relative to where they are. This is helpful for animals that hunt prey.

A MEAT-EATING DINOSAUR

The velociraptor was a meat-eating dinosaur, or a **carnivore**. It likely ate anything it could sink its teeth and claws into. It definitely ate protoceratopses and duck-billed dinosaurs called hadrosaurs, though. Paleontologists know this because they have found velociraptor skeletons fossilized in fighting positions with these dinosaurs!

This velociraptor is fighting with a protoceratops. The fossil that shows the remains of a battle like this one is called the Fighting Dinosaurs.

Velociraptors used their quickness, sharp claws, and their teeth to hunt and kill dinosaurs much larger than they were.

The most famous fossilized example of a velociraptor fighting another dinosaur is at the American Museum of Natural History, in New York City. This fossil was found in 1971, in the Gobi Desert. The velociraptor is seen sinking its retractable claw into the protoceratops's neck. The protoceratops seems to have fought back by biting and breaking one of the velociraptor's front legs!

HUNTING IN PACKS

Paleontologists think that the velociraptor hunted in packs. They think this because fossilized velociraptor remains are often found in small groups. This tells scientists that the group of dinosaurs likely died at the same time.

Hunting in packs would have been a smart move for these small carnivores. By working together, a group of velociraptors could chase and surround prey. This would have let the pack kill a larger dinosaur much faster and more easily than could a velociraptor that was hunting by itself.

Hunting in packs helped velociraptors and their relatives take down prey, such as this ankylosaur.

LIKE A BIRD YET STILL A REPTILE

Velociraptors and other dromaeosaurs were related to archaeopteryxes, which many scientists think were ancestors of modern birds. Some even think they were the first true birds.

The velociraptor was a reptile, as were all other dinosaurs. Like other dinosaurs and many of today's reptiles and birds, velociraptors hatched from eggs. Many dinosaur species left their eggs once they were laid. However, there are fossil clues that show that velociraptors built nests and tended to their eggs.

Velociraptors had feathers and hollow bones, as do birds today. These two facts suggest that velociraptors had things in common with modern birds as well as with modern lizards.

NO BONES ABOUT IT

Paleontologist H. F. Osborn found the first velociraptor fossil in Mongolia in 1924. Since that time about a dozen more velociraptor fossils have been found.

Paleontologists carefully remove the velociraptor fossils from the sandstone in which they were found. They may use special glue on the bones to hold them

DINO BITE

The fossils of two hatchling, or newborn, velociraptors were found near the nest of another species of dinosaur. It is thought that the hatchlings were that dinosaur's meal!

together with a supporting amount of rock. This keeps the fossil from getting damaged before it reaches the lab. In the lab, paleontologists study the fossils before preparing them for a museum exhibit. Each new velociraptor fossil that is found is a chance to uncover more clues about the life of these long extinct dinosaurs.

GLOSSARY

carnivore (KAHR-neh-vor) An animal that eats other animals.

extinct (ik-STINGKT) No longer existing.

fossils (FO-sulz) The hardened remains of dead animals or plants.

ligaments (LIH-guh-ments) Tissues in the body that join bones to other bones.

mates (MAYTS) Partners for making babies.

paleontologists (pay-lee-on-TAH-luh-jists) People who study things that lived in the past.

predator (PREH-duh-ter) An animal that hunts and kills other animals for food.

prey (PRAY) An animal that is hunted by another animal for food.

retractable (rih-TRAK-tuh-bel) Can be drawn back.

sedimentary rocks (seh-deh-MEN-teh-ree ROKS) Stones, sand, or mud that has been pressed together to form rock.

species (SPEE-sheez) One kind of living thing. All people are one species.

INDEX

C
carnivore(s), 16, 18
claw(s), 4, 11, 16–17
clues, 5, 20, 22

E
Earth, 6–7

F
foot, 4, 11
fossil(s), 4–5, 8, 17, 22

G
geologic time, 6

H
history, 6

I
ideas, 5

L
life, 5, 22
ligaments, 12

M
mates, 12

N
name, 4

P
paleontologist(s), 4,
    7–8, 12, 16, 18, 22
predator, 10

prey, 4, 11, 15, 18
protoceratops(es), 6, 16–17

Q
quickness, 4, 11

S
scientists, 5–6, 12, 14, 18
sedimentary rocks, 9
species, 7–8, 20
system, 6

T
theories, 5

V
volcanic activity, 7

WEB SITES

Due to the changing nature of Internet links, PowerKids Press has developed an online list of Web sites related to the subject of this book. This site is updated regularly. Please use this link to access the list:
www.powerkidslinks.com/dinr/veloc/